FIRST

IS

FIRST

BY

Nuby G. Courtney

WeekendBooksTV.com Publishing

A Division of WeekendBooksTV.com Holdings, LLC

-

Published by WeekendBooksTV.com Publishing, a division of WeekendBooksTV.com Holdings, LLC

P.O. Box 190924
Dallas, Texas 75219

ISBN-13: 978-0615618463
ISBN-10: 0615618464

Printed in the USA

-

TABLE OF CONTENTS

FOREWARD

There are three words that I would like to call your attention to at this time: control, influence and authority.

Each of these words describes an essential component as they pertain to the woman exercising the role of 'Mother' in the lives of those with which she is maternally aligned. A most notable and significant task, a 'Mother' is summoned to do, and be, all things within her lifetime; with the most crucial aspect being the provider of nourishment, caretaker and protector of her family's unit.

Oftentimes, it is not until mature adulthood that we come far enough along in our mental, physical and emotional development so as to cherish and genuinely appreciate such a unique and matchless gift from our Creator. As children, we are dependent upon our mothers for introduction, education and guidance involving the world around us. As teenagers and young adults, we strive to distance ourselves from our parentage so as to exhibit our mastery of life's fundamental concepts; and, to achieve our own brand of personal independence. Alas, as a mature adult, we have returned to her womb; as we

-

have received our own lashes of physicality at the expense of our own life's journey, and,
are now in a place to fully understand and accept their infinite wisdom.

Whether you have experienced all or any of the above descriptions; or, whether or not you have received it from its originally intended source, please be thankful for having a Mother. As you continue to read and become enriched and inspired by my Father's personal testimony, stop and take a moment to reflect upon the positive influence(s) that you have received throughout your life from such an entity. Moreover, take a moment to reflect upon the ways in which you may enrich the lives of those whom you come into contact, daily, that are in need of fulfillment in this very capacity. Listen with an ear of discernment, open your heart and sow seeds of fruition upon this land in preparation for a rewarding harvest in the hereafter!

Respectfully written,

Millicent Courtney-Ware, M.S., M.A., PCI
Chief Administrative Officer
WeekendBooksTV.com Holdings, LLC

DEDICATION

There are two women in my life who are still actively giving 100% to their families. My Mother, Julia McCloyn; and, my Mother-In-Law, Vera Martin are the two ladies that I admire most for continually giving of themselves. Also, the Father God sent to me, when I was five, a man that remained a true Father to me until his death on October 3, 2000 (Lovell McCloyn).

God bless your soul, Father...

When I completed the rough draft of this book, Mother held it and viewed it in her own way. On August 1, 2005, Mother went to heaven; and, is once again with Daddy.

I thank God for your long life here on earth, Mother...

PURPOSE

The intended purpose of this book is to provide the reader with unique insight into their own lives; recalling if/where someone assumed the role of 'Mother' in their lives... adding flavor and significance to their existence.

ACKNOWLEDGEMENT

All my love and devotion to my wife, Patricia; and, my children: Kaseem, Millicent, Jason, Stephanie and Danielle for their inspiration and the freedom to pursue my career and dreams.

-

INTRODUCTION

Things came into focus for me when I was five and experiencing the separation of my parents.

The years before that can be summed up, briefly in the words to follow. I recall surrounded by the typical family unit; especially during Christmas and other holidays. I was not allowed to stray too far from home to play with other kids my age. So, my basic pals were my Sister and my oldest Brother.

I looked forward to starting the first grade since there were no preschools, then. Nonetheless, I started the first grade after my Mother and Father separated; and suddenly, I was in a different neighborhood with new responsibilities.

This was when I began to observe my Mother more closely; who suddenly took on new and varied responsibilities of her own. She would discuss almost everything with us; such as how long clothes would have to last, shoes, food and most of all, the conservation of utilities.

Mother was a Hair Stylist by day; continuing her trade by night. She worked both weekdays and weekends to continuously provide for us. We never curbed our appetites; so often times, Mother would make sure that we had plenty to eat. She would eat whatever was left; or do without, when we had consumed it all.

-

According to my Mother, My Brother left home when he came of age, began living with a lady then they were eventually married. Now, this left my Sister and I to our own devices. As you would assume, we had separate friends and always enjoyed the time that we spent away from one other. But, we also knew how to come together in order to achieve the common goals of children.

Mother continued to provide for our necessities as well as our desires. I do not ever recall missing a meal; or not having some change in my pocket, which led me to remembering Mother always saying "God knows what's best."

CHAPTER I

<u>GIVE UP? NOT LIKELY!</u>

It is true that we have all faced times, situations and circumstances that have caused us to feel like closing the door, drawing the curtains; or, writing the final chapter regarding associates, friends, and family members that you have repeatedly tried to help but found your tolerance level a little greater than you knew or ever imagined it would be.

I find this to be true especially with families.

In Genesis 7:1 And the Lord said unto Noah, Come thou and all thy house into the Ark; for thee have I seen righteous before me in this generation.

Also in Genesis 6:8-9 But, Noah found grace in the eyes of the Lord. These are the generations of Noah: Noah was a just man and perfect in his generations; and Noah walked with God.

While pondering the subject matter for this book, my mind was led in this direction; because the born-again Christian is a member of God's family.

-

The value God places on each member of his Christian family are exactly the values that He expects his Christian family to reflect upon one another.

Noah was not just in the right place at the right time. Instead, he was the focus of God's blessing; and thereby his family was spared along with every beast (both clean and unclean), fouls of the air and everything that crept along the earth.

Noah was special in God's sight, and as a result; he and his family were spared by God. Though Noah loved his family; he loved God, the most.

-

CHAPTER II

<u>DOES HISTORY REPEAT ITSELF?</u>

Were you ever told by other adults while growing up that you were just like your parents?

Well, I was told that as a child. I once overheard two ladies speaking in regards to me; stating that I would turn out to be exactly like my biological Father before me.

I admit that my Father was not perfect, and possibly drew a lot of criticism because he stood alone and did not mind hurting someone else's feelings.

Needless to say, the lady was wrong regarding me because I turned out nothing like my Father. My Brother and Sister will have to account for themselves in this matter, respectively.

On my Father's side, our relatives were not traditionally investors, property holders, heirs to wealth or God-fearing people, in general. On the other hand, my Mother's early childhood got off to a rough start being raised without parents from the age of 5. The Uncle

-

who raised my Mother, his Brother and their Sister all had their homes before I was born. They were not wealthy nor heirs to wealth; but, their children also bought homes and acquired good jobs. My Mother always prayed for a home of her own, and in 1966 moved into the home she now owns and occupies. Her Uncle and his Sister's Husband were Deacons in the church; and from that rearing, Mother brought us up in the church.

It is important to note that I do not believe history or tradition played a role here. I first heard of saving money directly from my Mother. Not just because there was little available for us; but because she could see future advantages such as a home, cars, savings account, proper insurance and planned retirement.

As Brothers and Sisters, we sometime categorize each other by distinguishing who is like one parent or the other. However, I like to believe that when we look at the examples before us we can see what's best for us, and set the best example possible for our own children to follow.

CHAPTER III

WHAT OTHERS SAY ABOUT ME

I taught church school for 17 years and also served as the church school Assistant Superintendent, a member of the church choir and served on the Board of Deacons and Trustees.

It has always amazed me that Jesus Christ, while here on earth, was concerned about who the people said he was before entering Jerusalem. Jesus Christ later taught his Disciples that he who was not against them was for them.

This fact, alone, has manifested itself in my life and resonated throughout my professional career, home-based businesses and private life.

I have spent countless hours reflecting on the type of impression I have made on others; rather than applying the thought Jesus Christ impressed upon his Disciples as previously mentioned.

Keep in mind that in Luke 9:22, Jesus Christ was preparing to go up to Jerusalem and suffer many things and be rejected by the elders and Chief Priests and Scribes and be slain and raised the third day.

My childhood was not filled with an overwhelming amount of playmates. Often times, I played alone at home. This was not because I was better than any of the other children; but, many times I found that other boys my age were attracted to groups and activities that I was not particularly interested in. Playing alone became comfortable to me. However, other boys my age would make remarks contrary to being a male; such as sissy, too soft, uncoordinated to name a few. These were boys who would risk injury and broken limbs even when their families could not afford medical coverage for them.

It was extremely difficult to avoid them; especially at school. As most children do, I did care about what they thought of me because it would lead to them saying things in front of the girls, teachers and substitute teachers. It was much more difficult at school than at home because I was living underneath the potential tyranny of their words; until I could safely retreat into the haven that was home.

Contrary to the fact, I played into their hands and started participating in games of strength and competition with the guys. At home, Mother was always cautioning us to be careful regardless of our endeavors; and, she continued to pray for us without ceasing.

Thankfully, my childhood and teenage years were safe and free from emergencies! Where we lived, if you had home-cooked meals, you were doing ok. We had home-cooked meals and it never dawned on me that we were not middle-class or above. Mother, alone, could not afford the things that we needed. Mother met, and fell in love, with Daddy who loved us instantly! His presence made a huge difference; and provisions were readily available with both Mother and Father working together to provide for our family.

Mother took us to church; but, Daddy was not attending with us in the beginning. Daddy provided a car for the family. For the first time, we had a car like other families in the neighborhood and it felt good!

Would you know it, I took on the primary duty of washing the car because our car would be the only car in the neighborhood unclean most of the time. I would wash the car when Daddy came home in the evenings just to have a clean car parked proudly at our home. I especially had to clean the car for Sunday mornings because Mother wanted it clean in order to go to church.

One day, when Daddy came home from work he tossed the car keys to me as I passed him in the yard. He told me that I could clean the car for myself from that point forward. It was then that he gave me my first car!

Mother, of course, was not comfortable with this new acquisition; and immediately began laying down ground rules for me. I was very proud! I wanted all of my friends to know that I had achieved a certain level of success because I now owned my first car.

I guess I wanted to know what others thought about me at that point. Well, I heard a lot of positive feedback; such as, "your parents trust you". No one ever knew that my Father had informed me that I had demonstrated great responsibility to him; and he felt that I deserved my own car.

CHAPTER IV

USING WHAT YOU HAVE

It is a wonderful feeling to know that God has provided us with everything that we will ever need to protect, guide, sustain and direct ourselves in this life in the beginning. It will become further evident in this chapter that regardless of the situation that we may be faced with, we each possess innate abilities that will cause us to become victorious over our obstacles (circumstances). My Mother always had a spiritual response for any of my calamities when I was growing up. At the conclusion of this chapter, I will share some of those spiritual responses; as well as some of the most memorable words of advice from her (clichés); which Mother referred to as "old sayings".

In the book of Genesis 22:1-19, you will find Abraham's offspring of Isaac. The young Isaac spoke unto Abraham, his father, and said "My Father?"
He said, "Here am I, my son."
Then, young Isaac said "Behold the fire and the wood. But, where is the lamb for a burnt offering?"

Abraham said, "We may read about biblical instances where physical instruments, along with God, adding the increase changed things and circumstances." A word from God changes things every time! Although Abraham placed Isaac upon the alter in obedience to God; God provided a lamb.

In the book of Exodus, you will find Moses in Egypt; and, later wandering in the wilderness. Moses Mother and Sister engineered a plan to cause Moses to be raised by his birth Mother in the Pharaoh's castle for the Pharaoh's Daughter; and was paid for her services. Moses received the best of Egyptian education; and, all the Egyptians respected and knew him well. However, due to the slaying of an Egyptian, Moses discovered from two Hebrews that the slaying was known; and, he fled from Egypt only to return at God's command after all in Egypt; who sought to kill him, were dead. Following a series of hardness of heart by the Pharaoh, the Israelites were then delivered by the mighty hand of God.

During their wilderness venture, the Israelites murmured and complained and God heard them; and took care of their needs, daily. God also established his laws with them through Moses on Mount Sinai.

The Israelites were a sinful people; and, continued in their inequities, for years, which ultimately kept them from entering the Land of Promise. Thousands died and were killed during wars with other nations; but, God would not allow the Israelites to be destroyed or consumed because they were his Chosen People.

Atonements were made to God by certain (chosen) Israelites for the entire Israelite nation. God utilized the 40 years to prepare Israel for what was to come. God wants us to know that Man does not live by bread only; but, by every word that proceeded out of the mouth of the Lord doth Man live (Deuteronomy 8:3)

Parents; and especially Mothers', utilize the pre-school years to prepare their young children for the things that they will face in school and in their lives. My Mother taught me when I began to toddle that I was to speak to others with respect and, to mind all adults. I grew up in a neighborhood where the approval was granted by your parents in their absence for other adult candidates to spank you, if needed. Then, when your parents would come home and were informed of your indiscretions you got another spanking! It did not take long at all for me to learn that there was something to the word 'respect' and to mind all adults, as a result.

Though the years seemed long while growing up, I thank God for Mother! She never gave up on preparing us for the future, and all of its uncertainties.

At age five, I witnessed my Mother and biological Father separate; which later ended in divorce. Mother worked to keep food and sustenance for my Brother, Sister and I. The pickings got thin; but, we were blessed to eat every day.

It was not long before my Step-Father came into our lives; and, made a dramatic difference. He became my Father; and my everything. We enjoyed our first family automobile through him. He added to our substance; and, God made him a part of us, and our family whole, again.

Daddy made the situations we had never experienced come into focus in our lives. For example, he would slip cookies to us in bed late at night after Mother had informed us that we had enjoyed our limit. He would also do playful things like come into our room after we were asleep, grab us by our feet; and then, pull us to the foot of the bed, just to annoy us.

At times, Daddy would say to us that if he could not sleep; then, no one would sleep.

Oh! Did I mention that in the early years, Daddy drank alcoholic beverages? As I recall, God never allowed this to affect Daddy's love, and care, for us.

-

One day, Daddy stopped consuming alcoholic beverages altogether; and, joined church with my Mother. As you know, Daddy had given me my first car; and, further helped to sustain me financially while I was in college.

My Daddy wanted to attend a college graduation from within the family one day, and he did in June 1972…mine! He was proud because he knew within himself that he helped to make that day happen.

My Daddy passed away on October 3, 2000 at the age of 80. On that day, a part of me changed. I did not have to look far; for God was with us all when we were faced with the fact that this treasured individual would no longer be here on earth with us.

I realized at this moment that Daddy had left a part of himself within each of us. That piece was family unity.

Daddy really touched and changed our lives in a very profound way. He instilled the desire to stick together through all things and to rally around our Mother; while simultaneously honoring God in all things. God is our source all the time; and, we are to always and forever rely solely upon Him!

All of us were not born-again Christians. I am; and, God has enabled me to see his good works in each of us as we were faced with the fact that Daddy was now in the presence of God.

Daddy provided for Mother's financial future and his home-based small engine business had products that were later sold; and some were given away to family and friends.

Without God, this would not have been possible because obstacles and pitfalls were placed within our paths year after year; but, God has continued to give us the strength to overcome them, one and all.

We used what we had to overcome; but, God caused increase and favor on our behalf.

CHAPTER V

<u>SEEING IS BELIEVING</u>

We have all experienced seeing things with our physical eyes which required us to make a decision regarding whether we would place faith in the things that we have witnessed, or not. However, we should not believe all that we see with our physical eye.

According to Acts, Chapter 3:

Now, Peter and John went up together into the temple at the hour of prayer, being the ninth hour.

2. And a certain man lame from his mothers' womb was carried, whom they laid daily at the gate of the temple which is called Beautiful; to ask alms of them that entered into the temple;

3. Who seeing Peter and John about to go into the temple, asked an alms.

4. And Peter, fastening his eyes upon him with John, said look on us.

5. And he gave heed unto them, expecting to receive something of them.

6. Then Peter said, silver and gold have I none; but such as I have give I thee: In the name of Jesus Christ of Nazareth, rise up and walk.

7. And he took him by the right hand, and lift him up: and immediately his feet and ankle bones received strength,
8. And he leaping up stood; and walked, and entered with them into the temple, walking and leaping, and praising God.
9. And all the people saw him walking and praising God:
10. And they knew it was he which sat for alms at the Beautiful gate of the temple: and they were filled with wonder and amazement at that which had happened unto him.
11. And as the lame man which was healed held Peter and John, all the people ran together unto them in the porch that is called Solomon's, greatly wondering.
12. And when Peter saw it, he answered unto the people, Ye men of Israel, why marvel ye at this? Or, why look Holiness we had made this man to walk?
13. The God of Abraham, and of Isaac, and of Jesus; whom ye delivered up, and denied him in the presence of Pilate, when he was determined to let him go.
14. But ye denied the Holy One and the just, and desired a murderer to be granted unto you;
15. And killed the Prince of Life, whom God hath raised from the dead; whereof we are witnesses.
16. And his name through faith in his name hath made this man strong, whom ye see and know: yea the faith which is by him hath

given this perfect soundness in the presence of you all.

17. And now, brethren, I know that through ignorance ye did it as did also your rulers.
18. But those things, which God before had spewed by the mouth of all his Prophets, that Christ should suffer, he hath so fulfilled.
19. Repent ye, therefore, and be converted, that your sins may be blotted out, when the times of refreshing shall come from the presence of the Lord;
20. And he shall send Jesus Christ, which before was preached unto you;
21. Whom the Heaven must receive until the times of restitution of all things, which God hath spoken by the mouth of all his holy prophets since the world began.
22. For Moses truly said unto the fathers, a prophet shall the Lord your God raise up unto you of your brethren, like unto me; him shall ye hear in all things whatsoever he shall say unto you.
23. And it shall come to pass, that every soul, which will not hear that prophet, shall be destroyed from among the people.
24. Yea, and all the prophets from Samuel and those that follow after, as many as have spoken, have likewise foretold of these days.
25. Ye are the children of the prophets, and of the covenant which God made with our fathers, saying unto Abraham, and in thy seed shall all the kindred of the earth be blessed.

26. Unto you first God, having raised his son
    Jesus, sent him to bless you, in turning away
    every one of you from his iniquities.

You can see in this Chapter of Acts that the
Disciples, Peter and John were about God's business.
But the people who were in the temple recognized the
lame man's miracle and credited the Disciples
because they were with him, instead of praising God
for his healing power.

God is working in the lives of people known by you
and I today who were not thought by us to be
spiritually inclined when we last observed their
outward character. But God is calling on mankind to
believe in his word and not to ever possess doubt in
your heart.

As the lame man was, we must be a willing vessel his
obedience caused his bones to receive strength from
God.

Is your faith strong enough to know that God is the
same, yesterday today and forever; and, that he is a
rewarder of those who diligently see him?

(Amen).

FAMILY TREE

Family, according to Webster's Dictionary, is defined as a group of individuals living under one roof, and under one head of household. It is considered a group of persons of common ancestry; as well as a social unit usually consisting of one or two parents, and their children.

On the other hand, the bible addresses family from Genesis, and throughout the bible.

There are a lot of complex issues within, and surrounding families. Psychological and philosophical writers have researched and written about family genetics seeking to find answers for the complexities of families.

The Bible addresses it best in Genesis 8:15-16, and God spoke unto Noah, saying, go forth of the Ark, thou, and thou wife, and thy son's wives with thee. In these verses, God took fervent steps to preserve the family.

Genesis 9:1- And God blessed Noah, and his sons, and said unto them, be fruitful, and multiply, and replenish the earth.

Within our family, I am not aware of any generational customs or traditions that have been carried forth. What was stated in the

Bible was good enough for Mother. As a result, I have ultimately enjoyed the comforts, and benefits of a family connection.

We may not all sit at the same table for a major holiday meal; but, by and large, we are an American family who has experienced both setbacks and, God's grace and glory. Not all setbacks were invited or contributed; and likewise, God's grace and glory were not earned, either. It was given to us; borne out of his unconditional love for his children.

John 3:16 states for God so loved the world, that he gave his only begotten son, that whosoever believeth in him should not perish; but, have everlasting life.

This tells me that God is very big on relationships! God sacrificed The One (his son) for the many (all people of the world). I have heard it both stated and read that to know God is the beginning of knowledge. God is my Mother's family foundation; and now, He is mine.

My Mother's Uncle (Joe Spriggs), who raised her, was a Deacon of the church he attended. Mother was brought up in the church because her Uncle Joe took everyone to church. Thus,

Mother always took us to church. I am very proud that she did as I became an Ordained Deacon in the very church that I was raised up in as a child.

John 3:16 was taken from the Holy Bible, Authorized King James Version
World Bible Publishers, Iowa Falls, Iowa

-

Family Tree

Charlie Spriggs
Joseph Spriggs
Josephine Spriggs
Nuby Bradley
Anner Spriggs
Emma Francew
Dency Spriggs
Dalsy Bradley
Emily Fletcher
Fredie Spriggs
Julia Nelsw
Courtney
Zabth Mcclam
Lisa Quade
Williams Courtney
Tuskee Courtney
Sonora
Josephine
Martha Courtree
Van Scott Jr
Linnie Wilsw
Fatina Scott
Anner Perry
Emelia Spriggs
Joe Bradley
Tess L Bradley
Pamela Spriggs
Hazel Sanders
Cora Brown
Addie Miller
Nelson Courtney
Eugene Courtney
Pamela Courtney
Williams
Joseph Scott
Selena Courtney

Names on Mother's Family Tree; and, her relation to them:

<u>Mother's Grandfather</u> Charlie Spriggs	<u>Mother's Grandmother</u> Josephine Spriggs
<u>Mother's Father</u> Nuby Bradley	<u>Mother's Mother</u> Daisy Bradley
<u>Uncle</u> Joseph Spriggs	<u>Aunt</u> *Anner Spriggs
<u>Uncle</u> Grant Ransom	<u>Aunt</u> Emily Ransom
<u>Uncle</u> David Spriggs	<u>Aunt</u> Freddie Mae Spriggs
<u>Aunt</u> Gracie Spriggs	<u>Aunt</u> Mattie Spriggs
<u>1st Husband</u> John Courtney	<u>2nd Husband</u> Lovell McCloyn
<u>1st Born Child</u> William Courtney	<u>2nd Born Child</u> Martha Courtney-Scott
<u>3rd Born Child</u> Nuby Courtney	<u>4th Born Child</u> Selma Courtney

Cousin
Joe D. Spriggs

Cousin
Ira Lee Spriggs-Hilton

Cousin
Ellen Spriggs-Johnson

Cousin
Rutha Spriggs-Facen

Cousin
Anner Berry

Cousin
Susie Miles

Cousin
Barbara Spriggs-Brown

Cousin
Hazel Sanders

Cousin
Wanda Johnson

Cousin
Berthel Ransom

Cousin
Ora Brown

*Denotes Mother's Uncle and Aunt who raised her from the age of five (5).

-

William Courtney, Sr.
Lesa Quade
Carl Courtney
William Courtney, Jr. .
Trudy Courtney
Sandra Courtney

Martha Courtney (Scott)
Julia Scott
Latrice Scott
Van Scott Jr.
Fatina Scott

Selma Courtney
-Went to be with God
at the age of one (1)
year, nine (9) months,
and twenty-two (22)
days.

Nuby Courtney
Millicent Courtney
Kaseem Smith
Stephanie Courtney
Jason Smith
Danielle Smith

-

Here are some clichés Mother almost always expressed to my Brother, Sister and I; from our childhood:

- What goes around, comes around
- A heap sees, but a few knows
- A dog who bring a bone will carry a bone
- Praise the bridge that brings you across to safety
- God knows what's best
- Better save for a rainy day
- Time brings about change
- Take care of number one
- Six in one hand, and a half dozen in the other
- A new broom sweeps clean
- God will make a way out of no way
- Money talk/Fools walk
- God never put a mouth here that he could not feed
- Don't let any grass grow under your feet
- Where there is a will, there is a way
- Where there is smoke, there is fire

In addition to what Mother expressed, I heard on a local radio station KAAY, a program where the disc jockey, Craig O'Neal encouraged callers to phone in expressions they had heard throughout their lives from their Parents,
Grandparents, etc. which I recall he referred to as 'old sayings'.

Craig O'Neal is no longer employed by KAAY Radio, but he is employed by a local television station as the Sports Director.
I forwarded a correspondence to him regarding the list he compiled to include what others had experienced hearing throughout their lives.

Mother's expressions, through the use of her clichés, were meant to teach us life lessons. I do not think it is necessary to explain each cliché because some are self-explanatory; but, we understood the messages that she was conveying to us even more with each passing day.

It is good to know that she cared for us; constantly warning and informing us on life issues that she knew that we would face one day.

EPILOGUE

MY INSPIRATION FOR THIS BOOK

The inspiration to write this book came from observing, and listening to, my Mother. The things she continued to do for us in spite of what she said were indeed a blessing.

Sometimes, she would paraphrase the Bible; and other times, she would state to us what she learned and heard coming up as a young child.

The cliché that stands out in my mind the most is the following: "You better put first things first"! Mother interpreted this to mean that the things that have benefited your life the most should become your priority.

With this thought, God inspired me to write this book because I am blessed to have first hand knowledge that a spiritual Mother will never give up on her family.

Another observation of a Mother that I have also observed to have the same love and dedication to her family is my Mother-in-Law, Mrs. Vera Anderson Martin. She, too, is a spiritual Mother who stands in the gap; constantly praying for her family, never giving up on them.

Thank you for purchasing this book; and, may God continue to inspire you to always honor your Parents as I honor mine.

Blessings,

Nuby G. Courtney

SUPPLEMENTAL REFERENCES

The Holy Bible
Old and New Testament
Authorised King James Version
World Bible Publishers, Iowa Falls, Iowa)

The Bible Promise Book
Barbour and Company, Inc.
P.O. Box 719, Ulrichsville, OH 44683
©1985 (Mass Market Edition 1989)

Standard Lesson Commentary 1993-94
International Sunday School Lessons
Eugene H. Wigginton Publisher
41st Annual Volume, 1993
The Standard Publishing Company
Division of Standex International Corporation
8121 Hamilton Avenue, Cincinatti, OH 45231
Printed in USA

Standard Lesson Commentary 1989-90
37th Annual Volume

Standard Lesson Commentary 1988-89
36th Annual Volume

Holy Bible
King James Version Gift & Award Bible, Revised
©2002 by Zondervan

-

Holy Bible
King James Version-Red Letter Edition
(Beautifully illustrated with many of the world's most cherished
paintings)
A Regency Bible
©1971 Royal Publishers, Inc.

Webster's New Collegiate Dictionary (A. Merriam-Webster)
©1973 G&C Merriam Co., Springfield, Massachusetts
USA

-

www.ingramcontent.com/pod-product-compliance
Lightning Source LLC
Chambersburg PA
CBHW020443030426
42337CB00014B/1375